Aggressive In-Line Skating

by Anne T. McKenna

CAPSTONE
HIGH/LOW BOOKS
an imprint of Capstone Press
Mankato, Minnesota

Capstone High/Low Books are published by Capstone Press
818 North Willow Street, Mankato, Minnesota 56001
http://www.capstone-press.com

Library of Congress Cataloging-in-Publication Data
McKenna, A.T.
    Aggressive in-line skating/by Anne T. McKenna
    p. cm.—(Extreme sports)
    Includes bibliographical references (p. 44) and index.
    Summary: Describes the history, equipment, and safety measures of
aggressive style in-line skating.
        ISBN 0-7368-0164-2
        1. In-line skating—Juvenile literature. [1. In-line skating.] I. Title.
II. Series.
GV859.73.M25 1999
796.21—dc21   98-45522
                                                                   CIP
                                                                   AC

Editorial Credits
Matt Doeden, editor; Timothy Halldin, cover designer; Sheri Gosewisch
    and Kimberly Danger, photo researchers

Photo Credits
John Lyman, 4, 19
Mary E. Messenger, 40
Patrick Batchelder, cover, 6, 8, 14, 16, 20, 23, 24, 26, 29, 30, 33, 34-35,
    36, 39, 43, 46
Photo Network, 10
Richard Hamilton Smith, 13

**Capstone Press would like to thank Todd Shays and the Aggressive
Skaters Association for their assistance with this book.**

Table of Contents

Chapter 1
Aggressive In-Line Skating

Aggressive in-line skating is a sport in which in-line skaters perform stunts. Skaters use ramps, jumps, and courses to do stunts on the ground and in the air.

Aggressive in-line skaters often gather to practice skating on different obstacles. Skaters use obstacles such as steps, curbs, and railings to perform stunts. Skaters compare stunts and teach one another new stunts.

Aggressive in-line skaters do stunts.

Street Courses

Early aggressive in-line skaters performed stunts in public areas such as streets, sidewalks, and parks. They did stunts on obstacles they found there. But some people in these public places felt the stunts were too dangerous. Skaters who lost control during their stunts could crash into other people.

Today, many aggressive in-line skaters practice and compete on street courses. These special places for skaters, bikers, and skateboarders are in safe locations. Street courses include many of the same obstacles skaters used on public streets and sidewalks. They also may include ramps.

Ramps

Aggressive in-line skaters often perform stunts on ramps. Skaters perform stunts on quarter-pipe and half-pipe ramps. Quarter-pipe ramps have one curved wall. Half-pipe ramps are U-shaped ramps with two curved walls.

Many skaters practice and compete on street courses.

Vert ramps have walls that point straight up.

Another name for half-pipes is vert ramps. Vert ramps have walls that point straight up at the top. This allows skaters to go high in the air.

Another popular in-line skating ramp is the spine ramp. Spine ramps are two half-pipe ramps placed back to back.

Stunts

Skaters do stunts while they are in the air. They call these stunts aerials. Skaters can do aerials on street courses. But usually they perform aerials on ramps. Skaters build up speed on ramps and jump into the air. They call this "catching air." Skaters who catch the most air stay in the air the longest. This allows them to do difficult aerials.

Skaters perform difficult aerials by combining flips, spins, and grabs. A grab is when a skater grabs part of the skate while in the air.

Skaters mainly perform ground stunts on street courses. Ground stunts include spins and grinds. Skaters perform grinds by dragging the wheels or frames of their skates over obstacles such as rails or coping. Coping is the top edge of a ramp.

Chapter 2
History

In-line skates were developed as a combination of ice skates and roller skates. Early roller skates had four wheels. Two were in the front under the toes. The other two were in the back under the heel. Ice skates have a single blade down the center of each skate. In-line skates have four wheels down the center of the skate.

Early Skates

In 1760, a Belgian man named Joseph Merlin attached wooden spools to the soles of his shoes. He was trying to find a way to skate in

Inventors created in-line skates to work like ice skates.

warm weather. But Merlin's skates did not work well. He could not turn or stop on them.

In 1849, Louis Legrange of France made a pair of in-line skates for a character in an opera. The opera character was supposed to be on ice skates. Legrange used spools as wheels. But Legrange's skates had the same problems Merlin's skates had. The actor could not turn or stop.

In 1863, James L. Plimpton of New York invented modern roller skates. He mounted two sets of wooden wheels on a pair of shoes. He placed rubber pads on the wheels so they would turn easily. Plimpton also built the first roller rink in New York City. Roller skating became more popular with Plimpton's invention.

Rollerblades

In 1980, a group of ice hockey players in Minnesota wanted to practice during the summer. Scott and Brennan Olson developed Rollerblades to help them. Rollerblades have a

In-line skates became popular with hockey players.

line of four wheels on the bottom of a padded
boot. Rollerblades handle much like ice skates.
These were the first in-line skates.

Other people and companies began making
in-line skates. The skates became popular
training tools for hockey players and snow
skiers. Later, people who wanted new ways to
exercise started using the skates. Soon, people

began holding in-line skating races. Skaters reached speeds of 25 miles (40 kilometers) per hour on flat surfaces. They reached speeds of 55 miles (89 kilometers) per hour skating down hills.

Aggressive In-Line Skating

Aggressive in-line skating developed as an organized sport during the early 1990s. Equipment manufacturers and other companies held aggressive in-line skating competitions.

In 1994, a group of in-line skaters formed the Aggressive Skaters Association (ASA). The ASA developed rules for aggressive in-line skating competition and equipment. It also governed most aggressive in-line skating competitions.

The ASA is the only international aggressive skaters group today. Anyone can become a member of the ASA.

Aggressive in-line skating developed as an organized sport during the early 1990s.

Chapter 3
Competition

There are two kinds of aggressive in-line skating events. They are street events and vert events.

Street skaters compete on street courses. They do aerials and surface stunts on objects such as ramps and rails. Skaters have a certain amount of time to complete as many stunts as they can. Judges award points to skaters based on the number, difficulty, and variety of stunts they do. Judges also award points to skaters who use many different obstacles.

Vert skaters perform stunts on vert ramps or on spine ramps. They also have a certain

Street skaters use obstacles to do stunts.

amount of time to do as many stunts as they can. Judges also award vert skaters points based on the number, difficulty, and variety of stunts they perform. Judges award extra points to skaters who catch the most air.

Some vert competitions involve teams. Two skaters work together in vert doubles competitions. Three skaters work together in vert triples competitions. Teams of skaters in these events perform routines. Routines are planned sets of stunts. Judges award teams points based on how well they skate and perform routines.

X-Games

The best known aggressive in-line skating competition is part of the X-Games. The X-Games is hosted each year by the ESPN television network. The X-Games was once called the Extreme Games. Athletes at the X-Games compete in different extreme sports.

One of the first major aggressive in-line skating competitions was part of the 1995

Vert doubles competitions feature teams of two skaters.

Extreme Games. The competition included vert ramp events for men and women. It also included a street event for men. There was no street event for women at this first competition.

ASA Amateur Circuit

In 1997, the ASA formed the amateur circuit for less experienced skaters. A circuit is a series of competitions. The amateur circuit allows skaters of different skill levels to compete against skaters of similar ability.

Competitors in the ASA Amateur Circuit can compete in beginner, intermediate, or expert classes. Winners in the expert classes can advance from local competitions to regional competitions. Then, they can advance to national competitions. They have the chance to become professional skaters at these national competitions.

The best known aggressive in-line skating competition is at the X-Games.

ASA Pro Tour

Most professional skaters skate on the ASA Pro Tour. This circuit of events features the world's best aggressive in-line skaters. ESPN televises the events on the ASA Pro Tour. Skaters compete for thousands of dollars in prizes.

Skaters on the ASA Pro Tour receive rankings based on their performances in tour events. Skaters with the highest rankings compete at the ASA World Championships and the X-Games.

National In-Line Skate Series

The National In-Line Skate Series (NISS) is another series of aggressive in-line skating competitions. There are six to 10 NISS events each year. The skater who scores the most points in all the events is the NISS champion.

NISS events are mainly for amateur skaters. But a few professional skaters compete in the NISS events as well.

The National In-Line Skate Series (NISS) is mainly for amateur skaters.

Chapter 4
Equipment

Skates are the most important piece of aggressive in-line skating equipment. Aggressive skaters have special skates for their sport. Aggressive skates are soft and bend easily. This gives skaters flexibility. Skate bottoms are wider than the bottoms on regular in-line skates. This gives skaters better balance.

The Shell

The shell is the hard outside case of an in-line skate. The shell covers the boot. The boot is the main body of the skate. Aggressive skate shells are made of durable plastic or leather.

Aggressive skates have wide bottoms.

They must be strong to handle the stress of difficult stunts.

The shell supports the skater's ankles. It also helps to keep the skater's legs directly above the line of wheels. This provides balance and stability.

The Liner
The liner is the inner part of the boot that covers the foot. The liner fits into the shell. The liner provides padding and protection for the foot.

Liners are made of foam. The thickness of a liner is called its density. Liners with high densities are hard and stiff. Liners with low densities are soft and bend easily. Most aggressive skaters prefer high-density liners. High-density liners give skaters the best control of their skates.

Frames
The frame of the skate connects the boot to the wheels. The frame is also called the chassis. Frames are made of hard plastic or metal.

Aggressive skates must be strong to handle stunts such as grinds.

Frames must be very strong to handle the stress of aggressive skating. Most aggressive skaters use frames that are low to the ground. Low frames give skates stability. This is especially important to skaters trying to land after performing difficult aerial stunts.

Wheels

Aggressive in-line skates have strong wheels. These wheels are made of polyurethane (pol-ee-YUR-eth-ayn). This hard, rubber-like plastic can take a lot of stress. Polyurethane wheels do not easily wear out.

Skaters choose their wheels based on two factors. One factor is size. The other is durometer. Durometer is a measure of hardness and durability.

Skaters measure wheel size in millimeters. Wheels range from 44 to 82 millimeters (1.7 to 3.2 inches) from edge to edge. But most aggressive skaters use wheels between 50 and 67 millimeters (2 to 2.6 inches). Small wheels allow for quicker, smoother movement than

Skate wheels are made of a hard material called polyurethane.

large wheels. Small wheels also are better for grinding. Large wheels can become caught on rails or coping when skaters grind.

Aggressive in-line skaters use wheels with high durometer. Wheels with high durometer are faster and last longer. But they do not absorb impact as well as low-durometer wheels.

Wheel Rocker

Wheel rocker is the placement of wheels on the frame. Some skaters call this wheel alignment. There are three main wheel alignments. They are the rocker setup, the flat setup, and the anti-rocker setup.

Many aggressive skaters use the rocker setup. In this setup, the middle wheels are slightly lower than the front and back wheels. This creates a shape that looks like the curved bottom of a rocking chair. Skaters can turn and spin fast in this setup. But they may have difficulty controlling their skates at high speeds.

Most aggressive skaters use small wheels.

Some aggressive skaters use the flat setup. All four wheels are at the same level in the flat setup. Skaters who use this setup cannot turn easily. But their skates are more stable.

Aggressive in-line skaters do not use the anti-rocker setup. The middle wheels are slightly higher than the front and back wheels in the anti-rocker setup. Skaters gain speed with this setup. Skaters who compete in races use the anti-rocker setup.

Grind Plates

Grind plates protect the frame from damage during grinds. These small, rectangle-shaped objects attach to the frame. Grind plates attach between the second and third wheels.

Grind plates are made of metal or plastic. Skaters use metal grind plates to grind on metal railings and metal coping. Skaters use plastic grind plates to grind on street curbs.

Grind plates protect the frame from damage during grinds.

Helmet

Elbow Guard

Wrist Guard

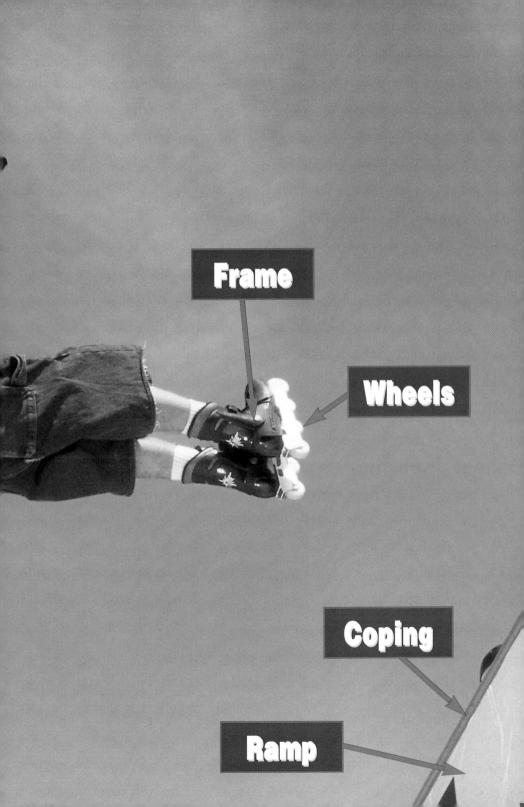

Chapter 5
Safety

Aggressive in-line skating can be dangerous. Riders must keep their skates in good condition to prevent accidents. They also must wear the proper safety equipment to protect their bodies during falls.

Helmets

Helmets are the most important pieces of safety equipment for aggressive skaters. Skaters can suffer serious head injuries when they fall. Helmets help protect skaters from these injuries.

Helmets help protect skaters from head injuries.

Most helmets are made of foam with a plastic or fiberglass shell. Fiberglass is a strong, light material made of woven glass fibers. These materials can soften the impact of a fall. They also are light and comfortable.

Skaters should use helmets that have been approved by the American National Standards Institute (ANSI). This group does tests to make sure manufacturers make helmets that provide proper protection.

Protective Padding

Padding is another important piece of safety equipment. Skaters wear pads on their arms and legs to protect them from scrapes and bruises.

Wrist guards protect skaters' wrists and palms. These small plastic bars provide extra protection to the base of the wrist. The bars help prevent skaters from breaking bones in their wrists.

Some skaters wear wrist wrap gloves in place of basic wrist guards. Wrist wrap gloves

Elbow and knee guards have hard layers of plastic over fabric pads.

provide more protection than basic wrist guards. They are made of leather and have a padded palm. The gloves have extra protection for the lower part of the wrist. The gloves are fingerless. This means that they do not cover skaters' fingers.

Skaters should wear knee and elbow guards. These guards have hard layers of plastic over

fabric pads. Aggressive skaters wear larger guards than other skaters do.

Some aggressive skaters wear shin guards. These hard plastic guards fit over the lower legs and protect the shins. This helps when skaters miss grinds.

Performing Stunts

Aggressive skaters should practice in groups. Skaters in groups can help one another after falls. They can find help if a group member is seriously hurt.

Beginning aggressive skaters should first practice basic street stunts such as grinds. They should master these stunts before they try aerials or other ramp stunts. Even experienced skaters can fall during difficult stunts. Beginners may not know the best ways to fall. They can learn to skate and fall safely by watching experienced skaters and by practicing. This helps them safely enjoy their sport.

Beginning skaters should first practice basic stunts such as grinds.

Words to Know

aerial (AIR-ee-uhl)—a stunt performed in the air

circuit (SUR-kit)—a series of competitions

coping (KOPE-ing)—the top edge of a ramp

durometer (DUR-uh-mee-tur)—the measure of a wheel's hardness and durability

frame (FRAYM)—the part of an in-line skate that connects the boot to the wheels

grind (GRINDE)—to drag the wheels or frames of in-line skates over obstacles

liner (LINE-uhr)—the inner part of the boot that covers the foot

obstacle (OB-stuh-kuhl)—an object that prevents normal travel; aggressive in-line skaters perform stunts on obstacles.

polyurethane (pol-ee-YUR-eth-ayn)—a hard, rubber-like plastic used to make in-line skating wheels

shell (SHEL)—the hard outside case of an in-line skate

vert ramp (VURT RAMP)—a ramp in which the tops of the walls point straight up

To Learn More

Brimner, Larry Dane. *Rolling . . . in-line!* A First Book. New York: Watts, 1994.

Martin, John. *In-Line Skating.* Action Sports. Minneapolis: Capstone Press, 1994.

Savage, Jeff. *Top 10 In-Line Skaters.* Sports Top 10. Springfield, N.J.: Enslow, 1999.

Savage, Jeff. *In-Line Skating Basics.* New Action Sports. Mankato, Minn.: Capstone Press, 1996.

Useful Addresses

Aggressive Skaters Association (ASA)
13468 Beach Avenue
Marina del Rey, CA 90292

ASA—Canada
131 Bloor Street West
Suite 441
Toronto, ON M5S 1R1
Canada

**International Inline Skating Association
  (IISA)**
201 North Front Street
Suite 306
Wilmington, NC 28401

Internet Sites

Aggressive Skaters Association (ASA)
http://www.aggroskate.com

Canadian Aggressive Skaters Association (CASA)
http://www.aggroskate.com/canada

ESPN.com Extreme Sports
http://espn.go.com/extreme

International Inline Skating Association (IISA)
http://www.iisa.org

Index